THE NIGHT WE SET THE DEAD KID ON FIRE

THE NIGHT WE SET
THE DEAD KID ON FIRE

EPHRAIM SCOTT SOMMERS

TEBOT BACH • HUNTINGTON BEACH • CALIFORNIA • 2016

Cover and author photo contributed by the author.
Book design: Gray Dog Press, Spokane, WA

ISBN 10: 1-939678-34-X
ISBN 13: 978-1-939678-34-8
Library of Congress Control Number: 2017930586

A Tebot Bach book
Tebot Bach, Welsh for little teapot, is a Nonprofit Public Benefit
Corporation, which sponsors workshops, forums, lectures, and
publications. Tebot Bach books are distributed by Small Press
Distribution, Armadillo and Ingram.

The Tebot Bach Mission: Advancing literacy, strengthening
community, and transforming life experiences with the power of
poetry through readings, workshops, and publications.
This book is made possible through a grant from The San
Diego Foundation Steven R. and Lera B. Smith Fund at the
recommendation of Lera Smith.

www.tebotbach.org

For Atascadero
For Ann

Contents

Foreword

Reading Ephraim Scott Sommers' bold book, *The Night We Set the Dead Kid on Fire*, with its provocations, torments and unsettling grace notes, I am tempted to invert Baudrillard's postmodern notion that the territory no longer precedes the map and suggest that in Sommers' hands, the stark poetry of self-making (how did I get here, and where, indeed, is here?) is all territory and no map—no surety of arrival, no resting place for shame's conclusions, no sufficient memory, no lasting atonement—only a welter of improvised actions, reactions, possible truths and reckless revisions colliding in a hyper-energized story space that makes the speaker's past as volatile and uncertain as his present.

> On the day Dickey and Landon die of heroin in the Taco Bell
> parking lot, you skate home shirtless,
>
> get lost in the hometown
> heat, stab a lit candle into a chicken
>
> pot pie and pray to the gods of dirt. On three-day weekends,
> more and more nickels at the park fall
>
> short of the fountain; each day grows
> older than the next. The clothes hangers seem to want
>
> to be empty, the carpet cluttered, the sun tea jug unfilled.
> And you can't drink your way out, but you will try
>
> a fifth of Jim Beam, two Percocet and rough sex
> with a pink bandanna
>
> for a blindfold, your first finger in the ass.
> In Spanish,

Atascadero means mud-hole, means no-way-out,
bowlegged or not,

no matter what buckshot you're carrying.
      No matter how big your dick is, when you wake up

every day in the lake,
      your heart is a sunk paddleboat,

and no one has a crane or a tow winch
or a beef-red Chevy strong enough.
                                ("Labor Day")

Sommers' dark fables of growing up in the shadow of alcoholism and inherited violence have a chaotic street grit veering toward nihilism, but his survivor's toughness keeps registering subtle, shifting states of mind—sorrow, loneliness, desire, love, the urgencies of forgiveness—that refuse anything as reductive as despair. Or hard-core nostalgia. But estrangement affords dangerous liberation in Sommers' poems. Rather than attempting to *fix* his speaker's shattered past, the poems play out the violent contingencies that endlessly make and unmake any life: "You're not America. You've always lived here. You'll always live here. / Here's your dollar and your brown bag of beer // and your cigarette. Now sing" (*"Hey Singer!"*). In "Watching How with Long Hair I Am Accepted by the Nevada Four," Sommers' careening images enact hazard's wild delight, "We come from where woman fistfight / four against none," he writes. "We are passionate about blimps. // The parking lot / of the In 'N Out Burger drunk and mock lit: / four adorable girls and I crush no one's teeth // to the green curb. We wolfpack the takeaway tray." More often, however, his speaker enumerates cataclysms and the resulting ways he disappoints himself and others. These are poems of complicity, the dense web of familial failures that begins with a single lack of empathy and ends in brutality. The unnerving power of Sommers' poems comes not from any one revelation, but from metonymy's accretion—the tally of damages

and the naming of ongoing harm, as in "First Confessional," a poem
recounting the sexual molestation of the male speaker as a child,

> I didn't say no. I woke up on the floor in whoever's back room,
> and no one screamed, *Rape!* in a crowded IHOP.
> Bless me Father for I define my body out loud
>
> in the shape of a crime committed against it...

or in "The Hardest Thing," a poem that uses the familiar wedding
question, "Who takes my daughter?" to explore masculinity and domestic
abuse,

>   and though metal against a woman's
> mouth is an almost impossible thing for a man
> to un-remember, and though across
> the courtyard, my Aunt Diane scorches
> a pork shoulder with a blow torch
> and spits Skoal onto the back of a golden
> retriever, still I am almost ready
> to receive the same father's hand
> that sixteen years ago drove a crowbar
> through my girlfriend's chin.

Although Ephraim Scott Sommers' smart, terrifying poems deny the
safety of *arrival*, they remain in their rejection of closure stubbornly,
improbably hopeful. Not for redemption or peace of mind—these
anxious poems know better than to hope for the impossible—but for
purposeful action after so much shame and wild mischance. The work of
a lifetime, converting sorrow into something of use, a song for the hard
journey ahead.

> I still believe whatever I uncover with a tractor
>
> trenching the town's graves for eight-fifty

an hour could be joy as easily as it could be sadness

so from these knuckles hums the mud hums the sunlight

so the sprinklers bow their heads

I open a throat in the earth

("Shovel Psalm")

Dorothy Barresi

THE NIGHT WE SET THE DEAD KID ON FIRE

Exhibitionism

Debra is a boxer, and the sex will be nuclear,
the kind I will catch Chlamydia from for the first time,
the kind her husband will kick the back window
of my Plymouth in for, but this is the minute
the CD Release Show is over, the microphones
have spit out their cables, the cymbals have been tucked
into their soft-shell beds, and my bandmates
and I are celebrating with whiskey. Because I never want
any moment I have lived to end, let me keep us here
in this one again before each of us breaks up
and hunches off toward our own privatized nights,
this one moment when my three best friends and I have built
out of sound a circus Ferris-wheeling across the country.
Don't put the glass or the hand down, don't let me go,
stay right here, where we hope perfect strangers might
touch each other under the neon lights. No violence
anywhere here, we are not famous, ours are not the songs
of the city, we are alive in America, and I never forget
the world has paid so that we can have a good time
all the time if we want to, and I always really want to,
so after we swallow and dissipate into the crowd
I find Debra by the bar, and it's the first touch
on the elbow or the waist in all that noise
when she and I first know where our bodies
might be headed, so the conversation seems almost
a trying on of a metaphor like a lime green cape
we could wrap around us, and we go on stretching out
its possibilities until we weave together the few blocks
toward the already agreed-on after-party at my house,
Debra and I, me and Debra and her long boxer's body
sparring with mine, and her strong, black hair, but waiting
for us there on the porch, and stomping toward us
in anger in the street, is my girlfriend, Trina, screaming

something like, *Your band sucks, and you're a shitty*—
but before she can say *singer* or *lover* or *human being,*
here comes the bottle of Admiral Nelson, let go
from her hand, the bottle I've been expecting
for so long, but before it hit, I might have considered
the women I've chosen alcohol over, women I've dumped
vodka on, lied to, screamed at, women I've crawled toward
and disappointed, women I've cheated or broken-
promised or drank too much with so I didn't have
to have feelings about. I am so afraid of dying
I'll stuff my face in the groin of a million barstools,
and as Williams began, *in a field of Helens, what could I do,*
I will finish, *but try not to fuck them over and fuck them*
over anyway? I want to tell my life as if it happened
to someone else, so of course I've been expecting it
when the bottle finds my face, and my cheek, the pavement,
and my blood, the bike lane, but then *BAM!* Debra cuts Trina down
with one right cross, and it is *this* possibility, the counter-
punch I *don't* foresee, that keeps me gambling, playing
these same hands in this same shitty card room, hoping
for the next unplanned and most pleasant surprise to sacrifice
my life for. For this brutal kiss, I'll go all-in. I'll forget
anyone I've been with before tonight. Trina's dead. I will die
this night, too, and so many nights after. I, who must frame
every memory of a woman in order to have a handle
on the world, won't wake up for a decade. It keeps going on
like this: Debra tows me into my house by the wrist, slips us
between the bongs and the man-cans, the dancers
and the Jackson 5 on the stereo, and duct-taping a bag
of frozen peas around her fractured hand together, and shoving
each other, bleeding, into my bedroom, we leave the door open,
our casket lid, so everyone can see what's inside.

Shovel Psalm

a squirrel whispers *thou art holy* to a walnut

all those other lives and their important sounds

all I don't know

I think about feelings for months before I get to have them

in the small business of my today a pickaxe after half a cold burrito

in the middle of March a foot on a flathead

I hear radio DJs large and far off argue nothing means anything anymore

ok I still believe I matter

I still believe whatever I uncover with a tractor

trenching the town's graves for eight-fifty

an hour could be joy as easily as it could be sadness

so from these knuckles hums the mud hums the sunlight

so the sprinklers bow their heads

I open a throat in the earth

My Father Sings Dylan at Sixty-Two

The old chorale voice chants, *Where there has been tragedy,*
there will be laughter, and I don't know if my father at ten knows it yet,
nit-picking the ugly dumpsters behind the theater where his mother
pawns him off every Sunday, my father babysat by the same movie
screen over and over until his mother's last-called or eighty-sixed
out of her bar, my father handing a half-eaten banana or last bite
of found hotdog to his little brother, my father shivering the curb,
and having had enough of being headlocked by his drunken mother's
drunken boyfriend, my father's scabbed hand finding the knife
and burying it hilt-deep in the boyfriend's ass, father hurdling
out of the apartment and never coming back, and now
at sixty-two clawing with me through a chicken carcass
and acting out the stabbing and laughing because he knows
our lives are the greatest of jokes, so why not laugh
at all fathers acting absurd with turkey legs or bowls of noodles,
or chili dogs or anything foodie, at our fathers slinging sandbag-
and-squid rigs into the ocean, flipping tri-tip or sizzling
pinch baskets of scallops or homemade jalapeno poppers
on the barbecue pit, my father with three teeth missing
behind his drum kit banging "Knockin' on Heaven's Door"
into the microphone, my father having lived through the army
and forty-four years on his back on a creeper under eighteen wheelers,
forty-four years of cigarettes and six-days-a-week and invincible grease
under his fingertips and dive-bar live shows and tie-dye, having lived
through a heart attack on Christmas day, my father sings Dylan
like a mystic hymn, smokes the live mic like a Lucky Strike because he's lived
this long enough to quit drinking, and we, his children and everyone else
in the world he never laid a hand on, listen, tearing into racks
of his secret-seasoned spareribs, the old family riddle all over our faces.

The Hardest Thing

No coming together without letting go,
Eva reminds me and reminds me,
for love, she believes, is two people trying
for the same place, and her I will follow,
therefore, into the future neighborhoods
of future cities until my elbows are
jimmied further open, for if forgiveness is
a backyard, she has taken down the fences,
filled the pool, and invited everyone
to the piñata. We are always gathered here
together as balloons so we may rise, she hums
and hums, and here her forgiveness comes
despite her jawline, her hair flowered
and floating the lawn chairs toward the stereo's
gentle question. *Who takes my daughter?*
Her father asks, and though *she* takes *me*,
though I've always said we were born
to get even, she revises my mouth to say
now we were born for getting over. She vows,
today, we will U-Haul up our memories
and send them away, and I am almost ready
to unlock like she has, to unlatch my fingers,
to uncock them and let in her father's
hand, and though metal against a woman's
mouth is an almost impossible thing for a man
to un-remember, and though across
the courtyard, my Aunt Diane scorches
a pork shoulder with a blow torch
and spits Skoal onto the back of a golden
retriever, still I am almost ready
to receive the same father's hand
that sixteen years ago drove a crowbar
through my girlfriend's chin.

Labor Day

On the day Dickey and Landon die of heroin in the Taco Bell
parking lot, you skate home shirtless,

get lost in the hometown
heat, stab a lit candle into a chicken

pot pie, and pray to the gods of dirt. On three-day weekends,
more and more nickels at the park fall

short of the fountain; each day grows
older than the next. The clothes hangers seem to want

to be empty, the carpet cluttered, the sun tea jug unfilled.
And you can't drink your way out, but you will try

a fifth of Jim Beam, two Percocet, and rough sex
with a pink bandanna

for a blindfold, your first finger in the ass.
In Spanish,

Atascadero means mud-hole, means no-way-out,
bowlegged or not,

no matter what buckshot you're carrying.
No matter how big your dick is, when you wake up

every day in the lake,
your heart is a sunk paddleboat,

and no one has a crane or a tow winch
or a beef-red Chevy strong enough.

Watching How with Long Hair I Am
Accepted by the Nevada Four

We come from where women fistfight
four against none. We are passionate about blimps.

      The parking lot
of the In 'N Out Burger drunk and mock lit:
four adorable girls and I crush no one's teeth

to the green curb. We wolfpack the takeaway tray. A blimp could end this
curb-stomping. We could stop,

rubberneck back, and O if a leaning blimp
would moon through this Reno-Sparks AM

thick with the thump of half-neckpunch,
half-*I-love-you*. The idea of a blimp is thick in us.
Only a blimp will do.
            We wait. We can't wait.
            We fiend new Levi's and blimps that don't show.

We hurricane inside and thumb packet-mustard murals
upon our foreheads. Then, as if from outer-space,

a mini-blue hand-fan buzzing in each fist, a man naked and thin
drifts in as if not naked, banks a soft-left at the restrooms,

    hovers before the register,
and orders a root-beer float from the secret menu.

Cryin' Bryan

I'm telling Michelle I saw the careening, rosy Honda
scoop up Bryan at the ankles, that I saw his head
dive into a spider web on the windshield,
how his body cartwheeled Olympic-like around
the air and his skateboard spun off and got lost
beneath some car in the Food 4 Less parking lot,
and I'm telling her, as he limped with one shoe
to a seat on the red curb next to me, how I did not
see him cry, not once, never, not when being axe-chopped
by a street-hockey stick in PE, not when his knee
dislocated on the quarter-pipe coping, or at the itching-
powder or testicle slapping incidents of 1999
in the lunch line, I mean fucking never, and I'm telling
Michelle all this with my hands as she perches above
me on the party barn stairs like a cartoon Pocahontas
dragging her wrist across her sour-apple-Puckered lips.
I'm telling Michelle all about the Bryan nobody's ever heard of
because I'm twenty-two, and already I've learned
praising people I barely know and saying I don't believe
in God is a way to make myself seem touchable.
Four-wheelers plow their voices into the field
while the California Valley yanks down the sun,
and there is no feeling like misreading a moment
of silence as an invitation to kiss. Someone might be crying
down on their knees behind the half-pipe again,
but everybody's gathering, standing with beers koozied
in the backs of their pickups, for another square-off
and will never notice because what's about to happen
is the shit everyone Friday-nighted all the way out here
to see, even you. Molani owned the Honda, dumped
the itching powder, Molani the Mormon with the Vicodin

addiction, Molani whose parents will later torch
their own house for insurance money and skip town,
Molani whose mouth has started fifty fights his body
never jumped into has finally agreed to one-on-one Bryan
at the party-barn with no cops around for miles
to stop it. The crowd circles, and since you're here too,
you know how a crowd can feel the violence
in the air like aerosol or a light rain on the back of its neck,
and as the first hands are thrown, it is the lack of sound
that surprises, and you bark to fill it, cheering on your underdog
or your friend, and as Lorca says, the body floats balanced
between those two opposites, suspended in hypotheticals,
and not being able to see over your shoulders for a moment,
I feel like Milton listening his way through a forest
hearing the poem of tall trees, and when you wiggle in
and get a view, I wiggle in next to you, and we laugh,
and after a few bump-ups when it becomes clear
that Molani is one minor clip away from asphalt
and my best friend Trafton from the side with a ten-foot running-start
flings his sledgehammer-hand to the back of Bryan's head,
we have arrived at the moment our sides have been chosen,
and for your sympathy, you're going to be some kid
going down in A-Town, in the night, in the human ring,
and I'm going to be one of ten locals kicking you.

Hey Singer!

Your tongue can't get rid of it. When you sing on flatbeds,
    you sing A-Town, on hay bales, on barbecue pits,
        on cords of chunked oak, always you sing A-Town.

All your songs about helicopters and hot air balloons

and train-tracks track back to A-Town, but you don't hear it.
    You swear you sing a thousand other cities—tent cities
        and cloud cities, cities of brick chimneys, windmill cities

and cities of apple trees, blackbird cities—and you swear your voice

has galloped all the railroad bridges between them, but A-Town sticks
    like a broken toothpick between your two front teeth.
        Your tongue can't get rid of it, like a mockingbird,

when you sing other cities, *windmill cities*   *windmill cities*, repeating

the intervals you've heard in A-Town's tire shops.
    You hear what you want, and you sing
        a thousand other names of only one name while you pedal

your bicycle around town, one name as you pry up railroad spikes

or fingerpick for loose change. After the earthquake imploded
    the brick jewelry store on El Camino, you never left A-Town.
        Your Thames is a dry creek bed off Traffic Way.

Your Empire State Building is a wooden crutch you found

behind the AM/PM. Stop pretending. A-Town isn't everywhere.
        You're not America. You've always lived here. You'll always live here.
            Here's your dollar and your brown bag of beer

and your cigarette. Now sing.

First Confessional

I didn't say no. I woke up on the floor in whoever's back room,
and no one screamed, *Rape!* in a crowded IHOP.
Bless me Father for I define my body out loud

in the shape of a crime committed against it.
So everybody owes you. So here's mine…I confess
to a memory: five-years-old and my sister jerking

my shoulders, yelling, *What hurts!?!*
What hurts!?! The world always wants to know,
and me not knowing how to frame it.

A marble is rolling down inside me from my five-year-old neck
to my belly and back again, me having just been tongue-
kissed by my twelve-year-old cousin in my grandma's barn

and feeling something like guilt for how good it feels,
the secret, the surviving, my silent pride. So I answer, *I don't know,*
when my mother asks, *Do you think a woman can really rape a man?*

Because who hurts the way the world wants them to, Father?
Depending on who you ask, I've thrown myself away
too often, I'm too messed up for a kiss to mean anything.

The Singer Sets the Town on Fire to Get Himself Seen

There are times I can only see the car-crash
happen in the crowd's face because I am
the car-crash, times I come up short, times
I come too early, spill too much, and apologize
too little. Maybe I'm only here to warm up

the crowd for the headliner, but *Shazam!*

here I am, hip-deep in the Gulf of Mexico,
unafraid of alligators and burning a midnight hole
in the ocean. Tonight might be a memory, yes,
but my town is out here with me. I can't see its face,
but I can still hear its song, and I will always

be so certain with only that song to go on, that steam

to wrap my fingers around like an Irish car bomb,
and sure, if it is a memory, then maybe I imagine a crowd
gathering on the beach, hoisting its fists to the air,
the blood swelling in its biceps as I mortar the night,
and puddles of warm moonlight balloon my cheeks

with being seen, but listen—

in today's tangible world, I'd eat broken aircraft carriers
and rocket-fuel and launch my Plymouth minivan
and anyone I've ever known off a cliff with me into the sea
to jumpstart this show and blaze a hot comet through

my loneliness. It's true, and whether everybody's watching
or nobody is, when I'm floating on my back
in the fire, I don't have to see my town's face to know
it's burning with me.

Trina and I at the End of the Earth

We are barefoot and ashing and stomping
our cigarettes into the bottle-capped carpet
of your Cedar Creek apartment. I'm afraid
of what you're capable of bringing out in me:
to want nothing at all outside your living room—
a glass table, a deck of cards, eight packs of Kool
Menthol Filter Kings, eighty Pabst bottles,
and a tangerine thermos with silver rum.
My roommate and I across from your roommate
and you. In our game of war, the winner
and loser drink together, will sleep together
and forget about it and laugh about it. Nothing
in this room is inhuman. We did all this.
You tongue my knuckles and dare me
to send them through your drywall, the same
care with which a sensei tapes the hands
which will later be smashed into cinderblocks.
We staple over our punches with red paper plates.
We'll be at this all night. We've gotten good
at slap-boxing, at lofting our empties
into the caked-dish kitchen sink.
When was the last time we ate, Trina? We spin
and spin the thermos until everyone has
tasted everyone's nipple or elbow, and Trina,
I should leave you tonight. How you smear out
lit matchsticks on your chin, how you pinch
a dip in your lip and spit on the walls with your shark's mouth,
how in your purple t-shirt and dolphin shorts,
you make a joke out of the whole world—
no skinny jeans, no earring, no rubber-band bracelet,
no television or radio or cellphone, no V-necks or Vans

allowed in the apartment, but I won't be able to leave you,
Trina, to stop laughing as you hang your ass over
the wooden balcony and shit on the sidewalk below
because you don't care if the moon is looking.

Typical

to across the cheek receive

the bottle's backhand

to divorce to shine the dishes

to sex again to replay

the familiar name

to put things away

to take things out

to ooze the bird heart

into a skillet though unwise

to pump the yolk until it pops

to needle the eggshell

with an abalone mallet

to repeat backwards

not do not do

Get Out of the Way, Ephraim

Don't apologize for spending your life in silence.
As a hotel phone hurting into the morning,

so many of your lives will begin,
but whatever I am now must remind you

also like an echo, Ephraim, that you are still alive,
that there is someone else for you to be today,

ice chests or friendship for you to carry and say,
but, Ephraim, first, thank the sky that people will wait

their whole lives for you to tie your shoes.
You are late to the bar but alive, and easing into a seat

at the Oakhurst Dive, you remember your mother
shoveling the head off a diamondback,

telling you, *Maybe something must die first
in order for us to find the words to call the living*

beautiful. Ephraim, stop talking to yourself
in the mirror. Ephraim, get out of the way!

Trafton's father, Tommy, has died,
and your band mate, Trafton, is taking off his face

at the wake while talking in front of the regulars
about his father in a way you never could,

the wind being trucked out of every living lung looking on,
and he's talking with the soft Godliness of fog,

the ceiling and so many of his faces leaking
into the pretzel bowls, so be more generous,

Ephraim, bend down, and let a man you love stand
on your shoulders. Tell the room your friend is

the best hibiscus of all of you in a daylight language
you were never taught to speak. Ephraim,

a whiskey and a bottle of beer have been sitting
before the two of you in this loyal and dim lit way

for as long as you can remember. Do not grow tired
of being unbelievable. So many not here will say,

There is not real love between two men
in a dive bar on a Saturday afternoon

where most people say, *There will be trouble*
unlike any other, but you must not believe them.

—Trafton, look up! Trafton, you, too,
and I shall not believe those who declare in theory

what they never prove in life. Brother,
I declare you ordained to praise,

alcohol or not, you, wading far out into the dirt
where your father was, you, shoving your fingers

into the deepest wound, you, the only son in Oakhurst
who's found a way to talk about the bullet.

Found

As a child, behind the house,
I crawled among an army

of caterpillars inching along an open field
at dawn. Like a hundred index fingers,

they curled and extended, curled
and extended, and pointed me

eventually to my sister's body
sinking into the scrub brush.

The pocket's kink-necked spoon, the head's
orange beanie, the artist's hollowed ballpoint—

Sarah's things—drowsed about
the wet meadow, strung out on needles

of grass. The dew lulled
on her blue tissue. A thousand funeral lilacs

and oleanders listened, each with an ear peeled
as my mother's howl overflowed the highest

corners of our marble church, but flowers
and bodies cannot fill the cathedral

like a voice, like recollection. The butterflies beat
at our screen doors even now. Let us let them in.

And keep them. And name them. Every one.

Who Is the City of I?

Atascadero Lake's face is a graveyard of faces.
An aluminum boat loafs dumbly upon her cheek: a blemish.

Weeds grow out of the trunk of a junked Cadillac. By a clot
of bodies—water, car, human—this is my body worn down.

I urge

like a farm-boy over-rubbing cob-corn in butter
for doggy style with China or Germany

in the bucket of a tractor, but I don't want to.
And I am a woman.

I am a man with breasts who loves a woman

with her head shaved. The sun skids away on a boat trailer.
Bats draw black circles on the mouth.

I stand for the length of a cigarette outside
the country of my sex.

God Grant Me a Room for
Playing Cards Against My Enemies

Not with an armful of lilies or dollars
for the dead man's family, not in fear
or sympathy's name have we come,
and not with arguments in thick marker
on cardboard, for we are still breathing

but without a single thing to say
about sadness. Ours are the sturdy faces
trained against wearing the weakest feeling.
This card room, this poker game I am
waiting for, this spot of floor I am standing on

upon which last night Orlando shot Damian
down dead, I look at all of it, now, all Damian
will ever get from us. Damn. *One minute
of silence*, the pit boss says, *for a member
of our family*, and the Pistons' announcers

from a flat screen color-commentate the whole way
through my prayers the Pistons *Cover the spread*
and *Cover the spread*, but then there's Damian's
Heat jacket hanging over the hook in my head,
the Miami one with the silver sequins, and then there's Damian

in my daydreams, booty-busting behind the dealer
with his elbows in, and then there's his laughter,
and what other than that can we be expected
to remember about a man we used to sit next to
at a card table? See, a capitalist, a callous bastard,

I can be those things. I can try to hide it. Men walk in
and out of here every night, too many to count
or care about, the future money on my mind already being
blown, the minute given for the past, long ended.
That tinge we feel is excitement, and one of us could almost be

ashamed when in sail the golden beers and buckets
of hot wings, but when the slippery decks shuffle up and deal out
another unexpected destiny, or buzzer-beater, or pussy joke,
there is no way for us to go but straight on through.
Forward, now, and into forgetting. *The action's on you,*

Sir. Here, there can be no more room for remorse.
Check, or bet, and as for the others elsewhere,
all the proud others may go whenever they want,
may Plymouth on home and stare at a candle or laptop alone,
may reconsider anger from every modern angle,

get paralyzed. Everyone who wants to can worry
about violence all they like and count on us being right
here, thrashing and crashing and trash-talking
against each other, going for the win, because nothing,
not even homicide, can stop us from doing the American thing.

Shotgun Christmas

If you don't believe in heaven, what then
is holy? Before dinner, your diabetic father
punching a syringe into his belly, fill your mother
with Rockstar and orange juice, fill
a wooden pipe with a squeeze of weed,
and she will have your father leaning back
in his wooden chair, laughing the tears out
of his eyes. Your mother with a dark tooth
up front, *cock-a-doodle-dooing*, palming
a stray punch sent from your sister to you
over the already-been-beaten beef, and the salads
oversalted the way your family loves them,
and the television's volume pumped. Your mother
covers your eyes with a biscuit to keep the cold
from your dreams. The eighteen-wheeler queen,
she's the hot hand in meatloaf. Your mother
would drag a boxed-up house on a flatbed trailer
to Baton Rouge tonight if you asked her.
But you're staying scared of the outside world.
Frost is rumored this Christmas Eve, and she's outside
axing the kindling, singing "Smackwater Jack"
as she wheelbarrows wood up the three front stairs.
And in she whishes in a wife-beater and pink slippers
and cut-off jeans with an armful of pine. Susan or Suzie
or How-Do-You-Do-Sue, she's got your father
kneeling, balling newspaper into the fireplace,
your sister whipping double chocolate malts
as punishment. It's past your bedtime, and in your dream
the clouds will crack like a ceiling, will suck you over
the barbed fences and almond orchards of a strange frontier,
will grind your teeth to a white dust something
like frost. You will wake screaming. Your room night lit,

Santa won't arrive in your doorway, but your mother will,
barefoot, in a nightgown and curlers with a sawed-off
shotgun dangling from her right hand. It will be
the most fragile thing you'll ever see in your life.

Psalm for Saving Your Life

Of gunfire, tonight,
Damian, in ninety-nine
minutes, you will go
down, and so many
who don't know you
will begin again the ordeal
of choosing how not to
care about the blood,
but in your hand, now,
is half a glass of bourbon
and orange, and I know
your tattoos well enough
to hold you, and in this casino
card room and disco,
the bass is a sucker-punch,
the poker chips are being
piled up, argued over,
and separated,
and in all this dividedness,
we are holding a high-five,
holding half a hug for half
an eyelash, and this poem
is a little box with wings,
and I'm always trying to fit
a life inside it, so I must
make meaning out of these
seven holy seconds
before the seven shots,
before the seven holes
in your neck and chest,
before ninety-nine minutes

melt like ice in bourbon,
and your body on the floor
doesn't climb back
into your blood, and this poem
and the paramedics fail you.

Watching a Breakfast Table in Butte, Montana

On the lawn, a country of mushrooms is becoming
elderly, filled with ear trumpets

    and hat trees, gramophones and golden night masks.
I am ten again. My grandfather tosses a bocce ball at a sprinkler head.

All around us,
lawn gnomes in plastic are caught mid-clap.

    We have five conversations left. A silver pocket-watch hangs
        from the hip of a gardening clog.

We ice-skate together on the pond at the top of a golf tee.
We devise Tuesday rendezvous in memory's future smithereens.

My grandfather lies down on the top of an ant hill and wakes up
as snow safeguarding the city, as my hands flicking a packet

of Splenda onto a cup of coffee and paddling in.

Dear Trevor from Fort Lauderdale

The one who kicked the baby out
of Aunt Traci's stomach and the one who hung

his wife from the hotel balcony
and the one who lugged Louise around

her apartment all night by her turquoise hair—
they are all you,

Trevor the new miserable,
Trevor the night manager last week

who elbowed Ann in the back over black dish water.
And this shit's been going on for months, I learned last night

for the first time over tuna tacos, and think of any small-town
man whose lover's been fucked with and what he might do.

Think of all the husbands of once-battered wives,
think of your tan Acura I man-hunted down

and the brothers of bruised sisters, the sisters who haven't survived
still so beautiful, the cinderblock I belly-flopped

into your windshield, your re-upholstered interior
I water-ballooned with pit-bull urine. I'm thinking

of all the mothers, Trevor, who are quiet, how, tonight,
poetry will serve you and me. With these boots and the spine

of this hardback anthology, I wait for you to bubblegum out
the back door of 236 South Mall Drive at 10:17, and when you hang

your left onto Lovell toward the parking garage in your server's apron,
punching something into your phone, that scar

on your forehead, a million broken lines will be there with me, Trevor,
and I will fucking destroy you.

The Back-Beat of the Sloppy Joe Machine

His hands moonwalk on water. We barely hear
Bobby P. We know he's there, spirit-like,
eight hours in with his perfect teeth, floating
    high above us in his kitchen kingdom,

    a groove-walking Gandhi in a rubber apron
        whirlwinding through a twenty-stack of soup
        cups crusted with dried Detroit chili, bald head
sweating diamonds, singing Stevie in falsetto.

You have not hunched at the sink and sponged
for a ten-hour shift. This hymn is not for you
or how much you don't notice. This is for the phantom
    refiller of soap dispensers, the secret detailer

    of overlooked linoleum! To keep the sloppy machine
        running clean, Bobby P., our thin Almighty, hunts
        down the fumbled cucumber wedges, the tokened
tomatoes, and the triangled wheat, and dethroning

    the cheese like paint chips by the eighth notes
of his hips, he hot-massages the hanging spatulas
back into smiling, and with a funky *Voila!* the dirty-dish
    pillars vanish as if magic, for again ours is the kitchen

chaos he abracadabras into spotlessness. Come one,
    Customer. Come all. Let us dedicate our thoughts
        now to the spoon, to who made the spoon the way it is,
and where a God like that must park his extraordinary bicycle.

Sister in the Family

If you are a brother or a sister and you're reading this,
then you know about distance, you know about redwood fences
and locked doors and fists thrown over the macaroni-
and-ham-slab dinner table. You're old enough to know
about soap-in-the-mouth for a curse against your father,
the rumbling of work boots down the hard-wood hallway.
If you're from a small town, then you know about the sound
of work boots, and coffee pots, and the diesel engine
warming up outside your bedroom window. You know
the sound of your sister leaving for Long Beach, leaving
for college without saying goodbye (not because she doesn't love you);
sister of the softball scholarship, sister of the Long Beach officer
assaulted, of the finger sliced on the throwing hand, sister
of the school expulsion, of the return home to work with a jug
of tomato juice and her uncle's lumber yard to pay back
her mother for lawyer's fees, to marry a man with one beard,
one horse trailer, and two DUI's, to move to Susanville without you,
without saying goodbye not because she doesn't love you,
and she won't come home for Christmas enchiladas,
and not because she hates your mother's monkey bread
or tuna casserole or key lime pie, but because she hates
how you happen upon a dead dragonfly in your driveway.
You know hate too. If you have a family, then you know
about distance between a sister with a cigarette and a mother
with a bible, and you know the part of you that hates them both
for that distance, that hates yourself for moving to a parking lot
named Kalamazoo for a desk and a library and each day
saying nothing as you walk in and out of buildings
about your sister and your mother to your sister and your mother.
But you've never stepped into that distance not because
you lack love, not because of your new job or the gym membership
or because of the television, but because you know space
inside the family never gets smaller. And who are you to change that?

O Hospital Holy

Must another love story end, and how, and when? Asthmatic, shifty,
and hood-zipped with snow ghosting the 2 AM Kalamazoo avenues,
Ann and I hunch and hobble the hospital parking lot
with our tube-socks soiled, the dead asphalt buried in dirty slush,

the automatic urgent care door yawning open, and we want
to spill our emergency all over the hallways, but insurance forms,
signatures, the blank faces of receptionist
cashiers cataloguing, monotoning, two photocopies, two keyboards,

an examined and re-examined ID, and as a wallet fumbles open
painfully from a purse to squeeze out an insurance card, the hurt
widens, widening, and Ann doubles over as if some tank-grenade
has detonated in her belly and is still detonating, its shrapnel spreading

heat beneath her skin, and I try to know that hurt but can't.
The plastic waiting
space waits for us, our faraway planet, our tundra,
our inhuman cement and linoleum upon which we are so fragile tonight,

and bare walls,
popcorn-acoustic clouds,
vending-machine potato chips,
Cosmo subscriptions and Sports Illustrated complimentary ballpoint pens,

cardboard-armchairs,
a vinyl ficus. How much for a limb? How much
for a heart? The fragrance
of fear windmills through us—the double-parked wheelchairs,

abandoned bandages, a scab left behind on a pile of gauze,
something human must have been here on this surface bleached
clean, the ceiling fans on pause, a band-aid on a bullet-wound, a man
with a roofing nail buried in his shin somewhere

on the other side of the wall, screaming, *Oh my God,*
Oh my God! Oh God, do you exist in the background
jazz behind Ann's last name read aloud, clipboard-
butchered as a nurse gurneys her away to x-ray, sonogram,

plastic-glass camera-lens ray-gun eye-scope, chrome probe,
and Oh God, the EKG's 2/4 time signature keeps the terrified
beat, blood tubed, IV bagging,
blue latex, all the ice water styro-foamed? The open-backed

gown has always worried us, and another automatic door sighs
open to rows upon rows, rows
of facemasked nurses scrolling IMs and emails, googling, double-
clicking like navy-blued machines mousing

orderly across giant plasma monitors, assembly-line like, quiet
like night-shift factory wallpaper, and in Ann's room without
her, I fashion expectant trenches, pile the sandbags,
fidget my sunflower-seeded pockets with wet fists,

prepare for war against whatever
chemical-celled, bacteria-terrorist or diseased battalion
will launch its assault over this hill
at the guts of my lover, and I channel-surf through

my hospital memories: twelve years old and my comatose
grandmother's colostomy bag flooding with piss and shit
and my family pretending not to notice, all of us pretending
not to know her black colon, but we can hear it, and my grandfather's

second heart surgery four years before, his first two years before that,
and then I feel *myself* on the gurney, diving the double doors
to emergency surgery, my skateboard-ruptured spleen at five,
my gasmask, my count backwards from ten, my wake up,

the feeling of my body having been intruded,
and I still must believe
my surviving had a purpose, but I don't know why
I must believe. Because it's already 4 AM now,

the flatscreen sleeping, ice melted, the Norco kicking in, Ann and I,
foxholed, dug in, holding hands and waiting on the enemy
I'll kill, she'll kill, we'll kill together,
or we'll kill each other,

so we won't have to meander the wounded hallways alone, and *poof!*
the freckled doctor crooknecks
around the awkward curtain to repeat *we are still waiting*
on the enemy. We are still waiting, and I'm thinking

of my grandmother's gurney reversed into her living room,
my family sardined in, the laughter from the gargantuan rocket ship
of her body forever an echo, a memory, a distant rifle's report
across a California valley, and I think of her garage to find jars

of gherkins, golf balls and elk jerky in, or a trucker's hat collection
deer-antlered in the hallway,
think of following my father outside, him telling me
about her death under the plum tree, think of my sister

squatting next to the half-close-eyed body,
fingering the dead hand dreamily, sister I tell everyone is dead now,
and I remember believing
the body a lake and the life

a wind brushing across its face and then *poof!*
gone, my grandmother gone, the three-piece suits climbing out of a limo
like grey-haired groomsmen, coming to collect, the old oak,
stained-glass front door closing, my grandfather moaning

a sound so dark it colored purple all the happiness
and Christmas-caroled-joy in the whole world,
and a clock fell off the wall the day my grandfather died
himself (twenty days later nowhere near a hospital)

from being without his wife for twenty days, the day
I would smash flat all two-hundred-and-seven Shasta-cola cans
in his garage with my sandals in under forty-five minutes.
If we could believe in God today in this hospital...

For a ten-second diagnosis, Ann and I have twisted
seven hours through maybes like mountain trails
diffused by fog until her diagnosis is finally delivered,
Your cyst ruptured, painful, but it will fix itself, the diagnosis

we have waited all night for, the fog coalescing
into a cave, becoming real, and we don't have any questions
in two seconds, any questions in four, and when we can't fathom any
and the doctor shuttles out, our questions grow down

from the ceiling, solidify like stalactites,
but the doctor has flown away and can only be called down
with an appointment now, and I have begun to believe the doctor
is a poet in a clean room reading surprising poems

nobody understands, follow-up specialists, computers,
signatures, prescription-pill bottles. We have survived
the hospital.
Ann dresses in her gathered clothes and drifts

to the exit, and I with her, forgotten keys, forgetting the wallet,
a few more forgotten forms. *Have you seen my cellphone?* The sun
rises procedural, melting the parking lot ghosts down to black
and white, the roads, ready for travel, the engine sneezing

back to life, and still look what we have been given to consider:
today, blooming across Ann's windshield, there are only two
lime parking tickets we must split the cost of, not colon cancer,
and one of us someday must die of a broken heart, but only one of us.

Ruby

Where the blacktop shoulders
the dumpster behind Club Soda
beneath a cloud of Menthol,
and the locals dip the tips of our car keys
into mini-Ziplocs of cocaine, ask anyone
who they are, and they'll tell you
before the next sniff, *I want to be the one
everyone wants.* That's you,
Ruby. And we'll ask, *Do you
know that?,* and *Can my key bumps
and I and a handle of One-Fifty-One
hitch a ride with you?* To which I'd add
to the end of desire, the place where
I could be the one everyone wants
and the one who wants no one
because no one in the universe can
black-dress and macchiato-skin
into Club Soda like you, Ruby, and hot-
shoulder-lean against the satellite
bar, shove a Red Bull into a red straw
like you do. All the long wall mirrors are
breaking their necks for a better look,
the pool boys overchalking, the spigots
overfoaming their pitchers of Keystone,
and it's all for you. How you can
kickstart the shitshow night just by silver-
sandaling into it. To get with you, the bar
grumbles deep in its jeans for the brass-
knuckles and butterfly-knives, for the face-
kicks. How nothing's sexier than someone flinging
a forearm in the whiskeyed parking-lot
light with your name on the lips. *Ruby!*

All the cash and cards and Coors bottles
catwalking in the air, I don't want to touch you
when I send you a shot in this throbbing
Fireball summer, I want to be you.

Memorial Day

For the battleship that loved
my grandfather through World War II,

for had the submarines
or the South Pacific sunk it,

my family never would've been.
For this day, for Lake Lopez,

for our bare bodies blooming open
like the mouths of yawning lions,

for this rented boat upon which we can say
we are not afraid of happiness,

for war has killed so much
but has not yet killed us.

Thank you, whoever you are,
for we have come

not to live forever but to be
joyful for a weekend. For you

who has allowed this, thank you,
for spring rising inside us

like a tidal wave, for the first
strawberry on my tongue

in decades, for in the blue veins
of my white feet the hushed thunder

of the onboard motor at idle,
for the lake alive with wakeboarders,

air chairs, and party barges,
and not a park ranger around

for a million furlongs and leagues
and fathoms, for the new season

of new skin, of sunscreen, of straw hats
and shades, of beer koozies and easy-ups,

of back flips off the boat and an orange flag
in the air for a swimmer in the water,

for the woman, our grandmother,
asleep beside her golden retriever,

for the both of them who will be dead
inside a year but who will not die today,

for the both of them floating
a pink inner tube out into the whitecaps,

for the both of them unaware
of my grandfather who is holding

his breath somewhere under the lake,
for the torpedo of his aging body

just about to breach the surface
and just about to flip them in.

Water Body

I can't remember America.
Even my sister Sarah is a town

somewhere inside me, a town
whose shores are caving under the weight

of so much water, a sinking black island in a blue eye.
Sarah is a people I've never known to go on living, a miscarriage.

Of course I lied. When I say she's dead, it doesn't hurt so much
not knowing her. Whoever my sister is I can't say. I've never known

Sarah of the neighborhood toilets and sinks and bathtubs exploding,
the fire-hydrants overflowing,

because Sarah is the name for every overdose I've lowered
into Pine Mountain Cemetery,

the name for every warning, and with rainwater everywhere,
the name I bury and unbury and heroin apart so I don't heroin apart.

And with my sister swimming in this town that never was,
and with water made from towns everywhere...

and with ten or fifteen rumors watercoloring the space
where a sister was...

—Your houses are made of rainclouds,
Sarah, your arms, of fog, your roads, rivers,

your gondolas, rain, memory, water, my water.
It is spring, sister. Do you exist? If you can read this,

call me. The eaves above the hummingbirds are dissolving.

Mass Shooting in Kalamazoo

These grey daisies of sky, these clouds: Mary Lou,
Tyler, Barbara, Richard, Mary Jo, Dorothy.
Let these not only be names I lay down in a poem

on Easter Sunday. So I am one weed among many
dead flowers. I am where it is the hardest to be inside this
almost spring as one daffodil drugs a hummingbird

into kissing, and the ghost of my grandmother barefoot
in her front yard introduces herself to a maple leaf,
then another, reaching each leaf with a ladder so delicate-

orange, and touching each leaf to her cheek, and sticking
a tiny white name tag to each, even though we know
what's coming, what the coming autumn will do,

how for these monumental deaths each year, we will
never receive justification. Kalamazoo, even now,
in blunt sunshine, a valley of cerulean overhead,

already among the neon joggers, each leaf is
being forgotten into a tree. Be honest with me.
This is how we save ourselves in the city: by turning away.

We are already turning away from silence,
that silence— the blood we are swallowing—
that silence of my father against the maple tree

the day his mother died, a poppy crushed
in his coat pocket, that silence after six people
shot dead in a city I've only begun to love.

Wait. That silence we will soon elbow away
with noise is still right here. The world's
engine has stalled, and this is a moment.

Let me stay inside it. There is a great cloud
which is standing before me in the center
of this room in the center of any city,

and I have been standing here trying to shout
that thing away (forgive me). Let me reach
for the harder thing, to have two full congregations

of teeth in the cathedral of the throat
and not to use them, yes, this must be my impossible
human challenge, to fill this newest loneliness

with silence, to lie down on my back in the lilacs
with my eyes open, and to live here, and to sing nothing,
for when the whole field falls, a weed must not speak.

Partisan War Party for Mahalia Jackson

—"We're gonna sing and never get tired!"

If a bomb in a dirty backpack is,
or a beatdown, or a church-burning,
then a praise song, too, in which someone
in this world is certain of something,
is a political act, and look how mighty
she carries it, Mr. Officer, and carries on
coming over despite the history
of harmonicas, cotton and rope, the bayou
cud heavy in her country's blood.
Look how not only in the mailman
hunching down a hundred and first
can we see the burden of words
made visible in hundred degree heat,
but also in Mahalia Jackson rolling
a mountaintop into the thin refrain
with her two perfectly open hands,
and only when she slaps them together—
the one that kills and the one that soothes—
can I hear somewhere fifty miles
beneath the valley floor of the shadow
of my gut the two hands happening
at the same damn time, the liquid
I'd buried there Coltrane-ing
to the surface, and she's standing
me up, and she's yanking open
my body, and she's calling out
the volcano as impossible as belief.

Judas Home for Good Friday

I talk shit about God, and, tonight, even the rain
feels guilty, for it, too, knows, now, it will never be able

to stop itself. The earth crumbling out of my mouth,
what I know of heaven is a memory whittled from bone

and oak. All I've done is woodshed my church down
into a story anyone could call me a traitor for telling.

My mantra is not high-minded. I've never loved anything
that didn't hurt me first. I am the local rat on his knees,

knuckling a front door bloody, screaming, *I still love you,
Atascadero, you bitch!* while someone down the block

dials 911. *Let judgment come, or let me back inside*—such has been
my plea between self-display and confession, between a switch-blade

and a kiss, to those whose shoulders now hold the pews together
and to my past in the seven minutes before the spotlights arrive,

and I go back to jail in Michigan.

I Won't Be Able to Say This When I'm Dead

You know
I will get what I deserve for this—
Trafton's always been the sucker-puncher
who spent every evening trashcan-bowling
his rummed-up Cutlass around A-town
with the devil in his ear bud. He peed
on every coffee table that wasn't his,
and when the branch snapped like a skateboard
in the middle of the Mardi Gras party,
when he fell from a tree three-stories-
high, when he smashed two vertebrae,
everyone thought he deserved it.
He champagne-bottled my neighbor's right eye,
a scar forever, and bailed, and left me
with a broken window, with a mag-lite
in my bedroom, two cops rousting me
awake, two cops I lied to for him, to them
I'd never heard of Trafton, and now I'm thinking
about my neighbor with a scar and no one
to own it. I think about that face
Trafton and I didn't have to live with.
That was two weeks before he jumped
for that tree. I remember that same old Trafton
and all of us backing him. People thought
he deserved to be broken, but I never told him
when I came to see him in the hospital.
The words wanted to speak for themselves,
and now I will let them, the "get well" balloons
hugging close the linoleum, the room laughing
when he told us he thought he could fly,
the room saying I am glad he didn't get drunk

and die, and now saying we had been hoping
an ambulance would find him and stop him
because we couldn't, and now everyone
in town is waiting for a big enough fall.
Tonight, the Plaskett Creek campground
whispering behind him, he can't hear
my fist in my pocket, a key jutting out
between each finger. After eleven years,
I might finally receive some elbow
or foreign object to the eye-brow,
and I should get what I deserve for my dreaming
tonight I'm the best I've ever been,
and I've been ready to have my cheekbones
knuckled for that, but the whole campground
heavy-foots toward us, and as if I am nineteen
again, in the name of Atascadero and justice
and childhood, I duck into my tent
while they bash Trafton's face in.

A-Town Blood

I lumber down Pine Mountain at sunrise, shit-mouthed and scrappy,
my old lovers perched
like rabid nightingales in the bunchgrass corners of my chest,
my hungover friends fastening tool belts and waltzing onto job sites

off Dulzura and Curbaril and Atascadero Avenue,
undercoffeed, dreaming of great Pegasus rides to the dragon-heights
of clouds above a Chevron parking lot,
of great elephant ghosts, the overdosed heavy-hitters

of the past crouching over all of us,
the town's summer legends twisted, short-changed, the Monday
morning gauzed, our fathers coughed into retirement,
the what-does-America-have-to-do-with-this-commute-we-woke-up-to.

Some of us are already mixing drywall mud for the bathrooms
at the new McDonald's on Traffic Way or cement-mixing
and framing San Benito Elementary School's sidewalk,
some of us bucking thirty-two bales of hay into a gooseneck trailer,

some floating a spoon
over a candle
burying itself into a coffee table
next to a bed, a spot to nod off

for thirty-three dollars a night at the Motel 6,
but anywhere we wake up we wake up hungry
and hunting for more space to stand in. Some of us wake up
Craigs-Listing used VW bugs and buses on the internet

or foreclosed houses
or home-owners' insurance
while word-searching for blonde-on-blonde anal porn, a phantom buzz
in the pocket, a hundred and seventy-five photos

and seven hundred friends on Facebook, a fanny pack
and a yard sale, a banging of cobwebs out of the dingy corners
of the closet, a dusting of the garage, the furniture forever in flux
on the homefront, a deck half-finished, the hornets' nest needing

to be knocked down, the firewood restacked,
and some of us shuffle through the drive-thru ATMs
while considering socialized medicine
and Lebron James and Peyton Manning

and Sappho, push-brooming away the driveway boredom
to the thrum of the twenty-four-hour ticker-tape-news parade,
and in everything we ever look at we see ourselves and look for a way
not to. Hugging, handshaking

and high-fiving my drug lords
and my junkies, riffing into the Sunken Gardens with Rimbaud,
Laura Nyro, and the Allman Brothers in my earbuds, I wander
for a half-eighth of pot to smoke alone in a blue lawn chair

by the lake, to snagfish for carp
with bread-balls from a pole leaning against a blue lawn chair
by the lake, with a plastic bag of boxed wine, sneaking nips,
wondering who among us has already been let off with a half-day,

one thumb scrolling down my iPhone's Pinterest-infinities
in a blue lawn chair by the lake.
And who is already unwrapping a pastrami and gulping
a large lemonade on a bench

at the Paloma Creek softball fields,
reading the cement for hints
of drone-striked Iraqi children, I wonder,
who is finishing the day feathering the levers

on a John Deere, who is mini-vanning their kids home from school
in the fallout of Columbine
and Virginia Tech and Newtown no-beers-deep. Even Avila Beach
swirls and moonwalks

to the kelp-echoes of Fukushima and nuclear tuna so loud
I can hear it, and the statuses update each hour
to *soccer* or *Chardonnay* or *sushi and the gym with friends*
as I spray-paint my pink name across a Wal-Mart dumpster,

as I exaggerate myself a terrorist with an acoustic guitar
but admit myself a sickle-rich, farm-steady coward too. Wishful
and haunted, I push through rusty hinges past the vandalized
Atascadero Veteran's Memorial toward the Heilmann Park

disc-golf course where a buzzed joint whispers from hand
to greased hand, and the head-changes shift
in the breezed oak trees. Does that which happens to all my people
also happen to me? My mind is burdened with genetic-Monsanto-

factory-ripened tomatoes and fracked-sinkwater-spigots spitting
fire and gas prices spinning like slot machines, and money,
and the contests and competitions for who can tell
the biggest dick joke or has had the most blowjobs or money,

or remember the childhood half-nakedness of Triple Ponds,
remember the creek puddles behind the bowling alley
we rope-swung into, for who can remember newspaper
headlines on September twelfth or can throw a Frisbee

the farthest for money. One of us this day or everyday is
always waiting with a half-pint of Firestone Pale Ale,
sweating the present, the town creeks squeezed into dirt,
the day chalked up as sent-off, anxious, two shots deep

and blanket-texting while watching the town go by
from a barstool, and the rest of us are heading there to meet him,
the place we find someone to love being the same place
we find someone to drink with, where apples and salaries

and guillotined lemons aren't measured and argued over,
and in the only place where we can be that gentle to each other,
I stomp to the bathroom close to fully loaded, and the gravity
of America has nearly gone away. I wrap a dollar bill

around a pick-me-up and snort stardust off the toilet paper
dispenser, my head, a flying Fender amplifier for the cosmos,
misquoting Wallace Stevens and Robin Williams and *South Park*,
politics-talkative, mixing Obama with Baraka, new southern-

drawled, invincible, unbeaten, slipping in and out of an English
accent, friendly and back-patting, dartboarding and corn-holing
my way to hero, body-shotting with brown sugar
and bellybutton lint, backstroking the shuffleboard,

overly energized and forever ready to slap anyone or kiss them,
but we are eighty-sixed like always for swinging down
the hanging lamps or shitting in a urinal or ninja-kicking
the sink off the wall, so my friends and I stumble

shirtless, blacked out,
and leaning against each other into the small town loneliness
between streetlights
where the world won't go.

Our National Anthem

still there can be happiness

hearing its familiar

melody faint and far away

over the stadium speakers

outside the single-A ballpark gates

the autistic kid leans

into the wind

scrunches his hat to his chest

and whistles it

this thing we can almost see

we're all fighting for

under a shoplifted sun

in the back pocket

of a tiny year

Tornado Warning

Where tough and black coffee meet in Michigan
for tenderness and biscuits, I fathom the cord

on the oxygen tank screwed into the wall socket
of my father's nose. Wednesday. 4 AM. A cafe.

My cough won't quit. Outside, the wind is kicking
the teeth out of a birch. I count the breaths.

I wheeze. I worry tornadoes into a weather
talking so much shit I don't go for head medicine.

My father in my mind and fifty years of cigarette butts
enough to fill an airplane hangar behind him,

butts enough to fill the Olympic pool, and though he holds up
the water inside him, he is not a wall on a container

for sinking things. Though there are so many shapes
my hands can make him into, no metaphor is a father,

I know, and now that Atascadero Lake, held for so long
at the center of my childhood, has dried up, now that the creek,

tell me how to save in a jar what is already gone.
I'm eleven again as the music buzzes into my father's studio

below me, eleven again in my room with my ear
to the hardwood floor and the music Old-Faithful-ing in,

eleven again and already the end is all I can think about,
the part after my father and all his mechanic buddies

have lasered out the last neon leads, have thrown
all they have left of their throats into the final forty-storied chorus,

and *Can't you see... Can't you see what that woman's been doin'*
to me!? becomes nothing, nothing at all, eleven again

and already I'm afraid tonight might be the last harmony,
the last bridge and laughter, the last decrescendo,

and I'm falling asleep in memory to their cigarette break.
And I'm waking up at thirty-three with the cafe power

cutting out all over Kalamazoo, my cough burrowing dirty
into my back again, and the laughing

cook escorting his tiny candles around the room
like little life rafts of light. By their floating,

I fumble together my one crumbling biscuit
and two plastic jellies in a blackened cafe in Michigan

three thousand miles away from my father's hospital bed,
knowing no breakfast or band jam or bluebird

in the lung sings itself back together the way I want it,
and after this wind wrecking Westnedge, after so many

dead, do I somehow believe myself able to silence
this heaviness alone, to keep my father's evaporation

in California from everyone I know? Why when asked,
How are you doing? will a man never say, *I'm not okay,*

will instead look into his mug and say, *Can you warm me up
please?* I can ride this stubborn weather out right here,

waiting on what could be the final phone call,
and the wind red-lining against the windows,

the goddamn wind uppercutting the red awning
onto a distant roof, and a warning, a worry, and down

the road, a siren, a red echo of blue lights. Stop me.
I don't want to go there yet. I've been rushing my song

toward the big ending my entire life. Let us riff with this
a little longer, Death, my name is Ephraim.

You've been fucking around with my father,
but coughing up a little light, I still believe that he and I—

if we wake up every day despite the darkness
and bend to our good work—might undermine you,

and my father is a sledge hammer, a lion's claw,
an arc welder, a chainsaw, an impact wrench, and my father is

a bulldozer, a locomotive's lung, an upside-down mountain
made of wind, and he rolls on and on and on.

Us Sleeping in on the Fifth of July

An inkling, somewhere, of wind chimes,
and in the freezer door a spoon is cooling,
and this is the morning I'm almost where you want
me, Ann. I can sing a blackbird inside
a light bulb for you, can vanish the old man,
and with the smoking bud of an artichoke
can introduce my new self in part-edible pieces. Boil me
in saltwater, and dip me in mayonnaise
because my stink is desperate for the lavender
Tower Bridge tattooing your body from thigh
to armpit to barbelled nipple. All the blue
E-pills in the hardwood apartment have been crushed
and stepped into twelve hours earlier, and a breeze
tugging daisies into the sunshine whispers,
now, at the window screen. Will you wake up
and hickey me all over, nibble me again
like I need, Ann, because I've emptied and gathered
and sponged, because now I can juggle painted clowns
with the living things in my life? I've tangoed Pine-Sol
into the air and shocked the coffee pot back into breathing.
Look! I can balance with one leg on a red rubber ball.
Kiss my neck, now, and I'll turn into pineapple juice
for you. Interrupt my cellphone with a bowl
full of blue. Wake up and look, and I'll be someone
for you who'd eat meth shards or mud,
who'd knife your name into a policeman's knee
or seventy thousand public palm trees,
who'd build a piano just to watch you push it off a pier.

Forgettable City

In the seats beside us in Wherever-
We-Are, America, let us be honest

about our living mothers and admit
we don't feel enough of them here,

and I know why, driving home,
I prefer the not-talking, the highway

weightlessness, for I love to forget myself
in the narcotic I love. Call it paying attention

to nothing at all, not the city's torches
groaning to life, not the forgettable headlights

slurring together into the sigh
of forgettable silhouettes, nothing.

Each one of us is forgettable to the other.
     Think about that.

I want to be left alone forever, and then I don't,
and though there is so much rusty underwear

to laugh about, we are not laughing
together with our living mothers about our lives

this moment. No, not even whining. Just this
glass silence now.
     Just this drive through the now of night,

another living face I love let go of like a kite and lost
to some forgettable city's forgettable stars.

I stare hard at the present and wonder
if youth is just a gathering of lives in preparation

for our losing them. Still, to want to keep what is breaking
together, I should believe, is not a child's dream.

For how old am I if I am not yet ready to own my part
in the big untying of a people I promised

I'd kill for? A star should mean more, but like a sunset
or a grudge, family, too, it feels, like a house

on Mananita, is only memory, and whatever
the memory, it burns because I'm outside,

circling around the glass, hoping for the gap
to get back in, to drag my mother in California

back out, to gather us together in the present,
so we can tell each other once more how bad it hurts

being forgotten.
—And look, Mother, at all I will say to strangers

I won't even tell you over the telephone.
Just this now, this glass, this prayer,

and if this prayer really can put us back together,
if you can hear me, let me say first

the worst of it—Mother, it hurts forgetting you,
dismantling myself fingernail-by-fingernail,

inch-by-distanced-inch in preparation,
and, Mother, I can't keep returning and returning

to you because there is so much more
now for me to lose. I must keep returning.

Watching a Deaf Wedding in White City, Mississippi

beside a congregation of sun-umbrellas
the deaf wedding party listens

        as a woman carves her vows
            into a morning white enough to disappear a dove

I am thieving images

        I am thieving images from a dove-winged republic

     because I want to see in a language of photographs

what sound is
        how a woman plays an invisible harp

Talking to the Tomatoes in Susanville

one woman with a wooden voice can dig a long way

on a hot day salt seeps through my sister's sleeves

falls between clod and pulled weed in drops

a hailstorm of handleless spoons

across a land of incomplete boot prints

and so many weeks before seed becomes bean

or lemon cucumber or zucchini and seven more months

before Avenal State Prison releases her husband

farm hands before stealing the first taste

let their fruit ripen surrounded by this field's heat

where a dry tongue defends against a swallow

she is learning that she must hammer and hoe

and weed and water and shovel and sweat

this is what it means to wait for someone

Up Against It

We drink and drink as if rebellion has a body.
Never a wall around the outside world so infinite
as ours, we discover, and not any one particular gap
in the pavement or any one particular face, not the *Creature*

or *War Child* stitched across our hoodies, the day
we set each other on fire and swan-dive off the Avila docks,
or the way the trucks on the skateboard Trafton swings sound
against Adobe Dan's jaw, not our hands knocking together

which become for us a constitution we will stuff into our mouths
and rumble forward grunting. We drink. Never an enemy so infinite
as ours, and not how it will dump us into County, into cashiers,
into cement mixers and lumber trucks, into alcoholics or Afghanistan,

not how we never get caught for when we whisper a bulldozer
beneath the surface of the Salinas River or when we ease
a severed donkey-head into the public pool and call it a win,
but more the way we discover something named Adobe Dan is

a granite we can never be, and no matter how ruthless and cheap
the jeans, the knees, the bolt-cutters, the shoulders, the bones,
the chisels, the ball-peens, the paint buckets and the pipe
wrenches we throw against it, the fucker never goes down.

So we have played our nights like a game of brutal dice
in the out-of-pocket way, something has forced us to eat
our own teeth, and now we worship, finally, at the cup of gravel
and loss because submission, too, is a body, and it swallows us all.

My Dream of the Rescue Crew

There is a beige Chrysler.   There is a hole.
    We are the dead siblings, frozen

mid-argument in the Chrysler's trunk:
such brittleness
          and cracked windshields after a season of debris.

After a tornado in Tuscaloosa, there are sleeves to roll up,
but not ours.

Wash us. Stuff us with coat hangers and guitar strings.
    Bend out of us an embrace, some small mandolin monument.

    There is a hole   where our town once was,
        where my sister and I once were,   a hole.

We Drink, We Steal

What will we do with all the world's unhappiness?

Climate scientists predict headlights will unhinge themselves
from the teeth of cars and scurry toward the ocean. It is inevitable,

    and before the hamburger stand, a cold war begins
    over plots of sky. Our syllables like frozen plums are being flung.

        My town's clouds are better than yours,
        and something about sliced pickles.

We look at us in shop windows,
                our diamond kites abandoned to a drainage ditch.

Ann confettis our cable bill on the argument toward home, seasons
    the sidewalk with French-fries.

The loans are defaulting. Tow-trucks are crouching in the honeysuckle.

    How do two people pay for two apartments on one salary
    of imagination, tell the good-looking lie,

then kneel and clean the pubic hair behind the toilet?

The Dirty Tangerine

To spooning out our place in the twelve-story complex
as we would the space inside a pumpkin, to this our promise
in pencil on the guts of a grocery bag, that we have lived.
To heart disease and to history and to diabetes, to colon
cancer and Alzheimer's, to maybe and to maybe not,
for we must also learn to praise what may end up ugly
in us. Listen. The future has given us so much worry we hide
behind our well-behaved furniture, so why not dancing?
And not the my-neck-wants-to-eat-your-neck dance,
tonight, not the spicy unbuttoning with our backs turned,
the Nag Champa giving itself to the air, not the silk bandana
and candle wax kind of dance with one of us latched
to the headboard, nor the hot buttered tongue undressing
in the cave of the flaming mouth, no, tonight, we shall not escape
the festival of our pajamas. Yes, friends, this is *the* dance
and is, perhaps, our greatest adult discovery that not everything
of these bodies we share between us must be sexual. It is
the look-at-my-hands-and-high-knees-climbing-up-an-invisible-
ladder dance, a silent disco, a dance of imagined roller skates
across a stage of lettuce and peeled bananas. The before-bed,
put-me-in-a-tractor-tire-and-roll-me-down-a-mountain dance
because every hoedown could use a little mud, a little sawdust,
because the mammogram could go black, because the mole they pulled
from my shoulder could go malignant, because our dance is what God is,
that big, wet carnival burrito we've finally earned the bellies for,
that laughter, our blow-up mattress sitting in for a couch
and how when we climb aboard it whistles like retired pirates.
What I mean is that every mustard stain my lady Shouts out
of a cardigan for me is what God is, that a smudge of goat cheese
on my nose, God is not drunkenness now but dizziness, coffee grounds,
and dirt, the garbage cans stormed over, the bedroom abandoned,
a man in a lime onesie, bombing tomato juice all over the kitchen,

a woman scooping up the found skin of a lost tangerine, and God is
the dance of her thumbing it into his mouth like communion,
into her own like blessed earth, for God is also the challenge—
I won't spit it out if you won't.

Consider the Ocean

for my thinking is made from liquid
in sleep my lover breathes tidal against my bones

and hers are dreams I wish myself inhaled into
always I have had being without this body to consider

and because my father's cough is a storm swell

I ask a star from what coast sails the lung
which will eventually explode him

and the star tells me what has passed through
so much blue must stop passing here

I have seen my grandfather lost in the foam
and his Alzheimer's slipping between

my mother's fingers and her hair behind her
all over the wrecked sand like seaweed

for I am the shore where everyone I love ends

the brown of my mother's perm pulling apart
the three gone teeth from my father's mouth

fallen down and my sister Sarah is a scattered mist
I can't gather together   how long a crew must pass as one

through water before it arrives at its disintegration
is it the wind the crew shares or a family touching is it love

for I am so solid I am told I am so solid the star told
and what would I know of holding a thing not me together

I am neither ship nor ocean
I am the thing the ocean wrecks the ship into

Watching the Village of Atascadero, California

It is my old man riding a magic carpet
home with six bottles of long-neck Pepsi in his mechanic hands.
It is a husband and wife not dueling over footstools

in the living room, no flying wrists of wineglasses.
And why so hard to be these people, so hard
to be with people, so hard to people

this sadness? A blue man will find
melancholy in a baseball diamond, in a Capri-Sun.
Why so hard, elbow by elbow, to wish people happiness?

The small town talks to people it sees
under the raised red truck,
under the teal-flame '57 Chevy.

From the top of the Robinson's mailbox,
a wooden magpie bobble-heads in the breeze.
I too have ignored the only bird in town

that pukes a mouthful of candy corn if you spin
his head once to the left, if you hold out your hand,
if you laugh with him.

We Don't Die

—*for Heath Seager*

Maybe I'm a grain of beach always on its knees,
always saying to the ocean, *I give, I yield,*
but Greyhounded straight from Amarillo
with a wind tongue to kiss my worry

into less and less, you're not saying that,
Heath. After one of us here has wrapped
a drunken willow tree over a Honda CRX
and only broken an elbow, after one of us has

nearly died, we pour kerosene
on the sores, and you sing to the reckless
in those of us who go on living through
the car-crash night, who headache through

the morning after with scabs from a punch-up
on the middle three knuckles. Our life,
your record on repeat. Your voice, a jumbo-
jet on fire cannonballing into a kiddie pool,

a dragon hip-rolling into the doggie door,
a diamond of light whispered through a lattice
fence. Here, where I wish on a lottery ticket
for a wall of dreams without a hole in it.

The Search Party's Prayer

Amen is an end I will not say because I see
Trafton's memory in sound now, and I am a wall

in a cheap apartment to echo grief against.
As if he were a crossbeam, I'd keep asking him

how much more d-minor he could hold, his lap-
steel and its sugary, slow, lazy groan barely curling

an answer into the hallways I left open in chords
for him. Into an empty patio in a bar of music, Trafton

whispered a toothpick, a blade of hay, a suggestion,
so much air he'd never go all the way into. Trafton chose

to be the breeze, only heard by what it touches.
The poem, too, tends toward silence. It has been like that

with our lives—Trafton dead in California,
and my acoustic sleeping stringless in a Michigan shed.

A silent musician is neither hero nor coward.
There is being human to shoulder, we remember

this. There are wakes to stand through, yes,
and Trafton's end was Kenny and Jeff cutting him

down from the ceiling, as any end seems
some other silence to look forward to, the band

breaking up, the congregation dividing,
each member gliding solo down their own tired

little denouement. As an ear, now, a left-behind,
I must go feeling around for the sounds, for the prayer

of the next field where the leaning gate is
wide open, fence, unfinished, the melodies

innuendo-ed like I imagine Trafton's always wanted them.
Everywhere, feelings hang in the humid air like masks

at a costume shop for me to try on and play through,
and which one to choose for which song the world

sings me—the siren way off, the evening
plunging down, the train losing itself with distance?

How many lifetimes I've gone out, been up
all night in my Plymouth, looking, lifetimes

steamrolling and parachuting whatever anyone's got
if it gets me to wherever quicker, and I'm going

to keep dragging my body through this. I'm going
to start loving the worst in myself. Call it *going*

after the dead, call it *A-Town,* call it *ours,*
but whether I'm driving or you are,

whether Trafton's on my lips or your dead are
on yours, we're going to keep our restless heads

in motion and the pedal pinned because we came
here for a vehicle to get us to God,

we discovered our search was never finished
with us, and we are only beginning to live.

Notes

"In a field of Helens, what could I do," is my riff on the line, "Imagine you saw a field made up of women all silver-white. What should you do but love them?" from the poem "Asphodel That Greeny Flower" by William Carlos Williams.

"Tonight No Poetry Will Serve" is a line from a poem of the same title by Adrienne Rich. In "Dear Trevor from Fort Lauderdale," I invert the line from Rich.

Mahalia Jackson (1911-1972) was a famous and exceptionally powerful gospel singer. The line, "We're gonna sing and never get tired," comes from Jackson's performance of the song "How I Got Over."

The Sunken Gardens is a small sunken park with a fountain. It is located in the center of Atascadero.

The song "Can't You See" is by The Marshall Tucker Band.

"Watching a Deaf Wedding in White City, Mississippi" is an homage for Ilya Kaminsky.

"The Dirty Tangerine" is after Matthew Dickman.

Parachuting is a way to ingest the powdered form of MDMA. The user sprinkles the powder onto a small piece of toilet paper, then wraps the toilet paper around the powder and swallows.

The line, "A vehicle to get us to God," is my riff on the line, "Poetry is the thing that gets us to God," a line I once heard the poet Marilyn Chin say in a lecture in 2010 at San Diego State.

Acknowledgments

Some of these poems have appeared (in various forms)
or are forthcoming in the following literary journals:

Barnstorm: "Talking to the Tomatoes in Susanville";

Black Fox Literary Magazine: "Get Out of the Way, Ephraim" & "The Hardest Thing";

Beloit Poetry Journal: "Who Is the City of I?";

Cimarron Review: "Forgettable City";

Columbia Review: "Typical";

Cream City Review: "Labor Day";

East Bay Review: "Shotgun Christmas";

Euphony: "Water Body";

Fat City Review: "Ruby";

Harpur Palate: "Watching the Village of Atascadero, California";

Killing the Angel: "Consider the Ocean" & "Exhibitionism";

New Madrid: "Found";

Ninth Letter: "Cryin' Bryan";

North American Review: "We Don't Die";

One Throne Magazine: "Up Against It";

Paddlefish: "Watching a Breakfast Table in Butte, Montana;

Painted Bride Quarterly: "I Won't Be Able to Say This When I'm Dead";

Prairie Schooner: "My Father Sings Dylan at Sixty-Two";

Quill & Parchment: "Found";

RHINO Poetry: "Watching the Deaf Wedding in White City, Mississippi";

Rougarou: "My Dream of the Rescue Crew";

San Diego Poetry Annual: "Talking to the Tomatoes in Susanville";

Straylight Literary Magazine: "Judas Home for Good Friday";

Superstition Review: "The Search Party's Prayer";

Sweet: "Hey Singer!" & "Sister in the Family";

The Adirondack Review: "We Drink, We Steal";

The Minnesota Review: "Dear Trevor from Fort Lauderdale";

The Missing Slate: "Consider the Ocean";

The Nervous Breakdown: "O Hospital Holy";

Thrush Poetry Journal: "Partisan War Party for Mahalia Jackson";

TriQuarterly: "Watching How with Long Hair I Am Accepted by the Nevada Four";

Verse Daily: "Water Body";

Word Riot: "Trina and I at the End of the Earth," "Us Sleeping in on the Fifth of July" & "Tornado Warning";

Zone 3: "Shovel Psalm" & "The Singer Sets the Town on Fire to Get Himself Seen."

Thank You

To A-Town!

To teachers (Ilya Kaminsky, Jericho Brown, Nancy Eimers, Bill Olsen, Kevin Clark, and Matt Fleming) for encouragement, guidance, energy, kindness, and, above all else, time.

To writers (Franklin KR Cline, Glenn Shaheen, Michael Marberry, David Johnson, Andy Wickenden, Iliana Rocha, Amy Sailer, Emily Hendren, Dave Martin, Sam Deal, Rob Evory, S. Marie, Carrie Moniz, Brandon Lussier, Korey Hurni, Matt Morgan, Andrew Collard, Alyssa Jewell, Jeffrey Otte, Jeremy Llorence, Monika Zobel, Lisa Grove, Anne Reynolds, Lisa Hemminger, Gina Barnard, Rachel Kincaid, and Joel Cox) for help with poems, for arguments about poetry and books, for intellect, for friendship, and for community.

To musicians (Trevor Jones, Justin Pecot, Wyatt Lund, Isaac Laing, Mike Dorian, Heath Seager, Sam Sharp, Pat Pennyjar, Jabudah Crew, Kevin Thayer, Andy Wilson, Jake Moment Maker, and Rob Hart) for sounds and for all the late nights we filled with laughter.

To Matthew Sonnenshein for friendship, for proofreading, for advice, for brilliance, and for imagination.

To Tebot Bach Press and Mifanwy Kaiser for publishing my book.

To Dorothy Barresi for choosing my book to win the prize.

To Greg McPherson for poker, conversation, and free dinners.

To A-Town's Finest (Rory George, Dustin Hyman, Casey Robinson, Colin New, Cole Matthews, Danny Sanchez, Jared Hamman, Robby Busick, Joe Pat, Russ Monteath, Brandon Hendrix, Matt Smith, Zach Pearson, Josh Luce, Colby Bridges, Matt Torrey, Jonah Heller, and Jeff Hood) for loyalty, stories, and brotherhood.

To family (Mom, Dad, Shawna, and Sarah) for knowing what work is and illustrating it by example.

To those good friends and family we lost (Virgil and Barbara Sommers, Andy Marques, Cainan Tucker, Ryan Johnson, and Brandon Hamburg). We remember you always.

To gods and goddesses of poetry living and dead who have allowed me a place in the conversation.

To Ann, my life, my love, forever.

TEBOT BACH
A 501 (c) (3) Literary Arts Education Non Profit

THE TEBOT BACH MISSION: advancing literacy, strengthening
community, and transforming life experiences with the power of poetry
through readings, workshops, and publications.

THE TEBOT BACH PROGRAMS
1. A poetry reading and writing workshop series for venues such as homeless
shelters, battered women's shelters, nursing homes, senior citizen daycare
centers, Veterans organizations, hospitals, AIDS hospices, correctional
facilities which serve under-represented populations. Participating poets
include: John Balaban, Brendan Constantine, Megan Doherty, Richard Jones,
Dorianne Laux, M.L. Leibler, Laurence Lieberman, Carol Moldaw, Patricia
Smith, Arthur Sze, Carine Topal, Cecilia Woloch.

2. A poetry reading and writing workshop series for the community Southern
California at large, and for schools K-University. The workshops feature
local, national, and international teaching poets; David St. John, Charles
Webb, Wanda Coleman, Amy Gerstler, Patricia Smith, Holly Prado, Dorothy
Lux, Rebecca Seiferle, Suzanne Lummis, Michael Datcher, B.H. Fairchild,
Cecilia Woloch, Chris Abani, Laurel Ann Bogen, Sam Hamill, David Lehman,
Christopher Buckley, Mark Doty.

3. A publishing component to give local, national, and international poets a
venue for publishing and distribution.

Tebot Bach
Box 7887
Huntington Beach, CA 92615-7887
714-968-0905
www.tebotbach.org